This Book Belongs To:

_____

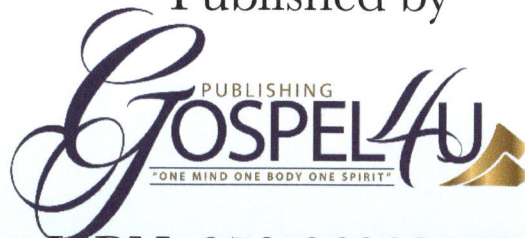

PUBLISHING
GOSPEL4U
"ONE MIND ONE BODY ONE SPIRIT"

ISBN: 978-0692355800
Library Of Congress Number: 2014922602

This children's book is about family and friends and how important they all are. The book consists of two different stories that will be very enriching to all children.

You don't have to worry about your kids reading my books. They're fun and full of entertaining stories to be read over and over again.

Hope More

I Will Get Better & I Don't Need Help

Story 1

When I arrived at the hospital, the doctor said to me, "You will get better! Just wait and see, and most of all, you have to believe."

Later on that night, as my mom stayed by my side, I pretended like I was asleep. Then I saw her crying. She wiped the sweat from my head and kissed my cheek. With a soft gentle wink she said, "You will get better."

Early the next day, my friends were there with no gloom. They were telling my crazy jokes as they danced around the room. They gave me my favorite doll and showed me my favorite team sweater. They called me their *little fighter* and said, "I will get better."

When I passed another kid in the hall, she was amazed at the wound she saw. Then she smiled and said to me, "You will get better, just like me."

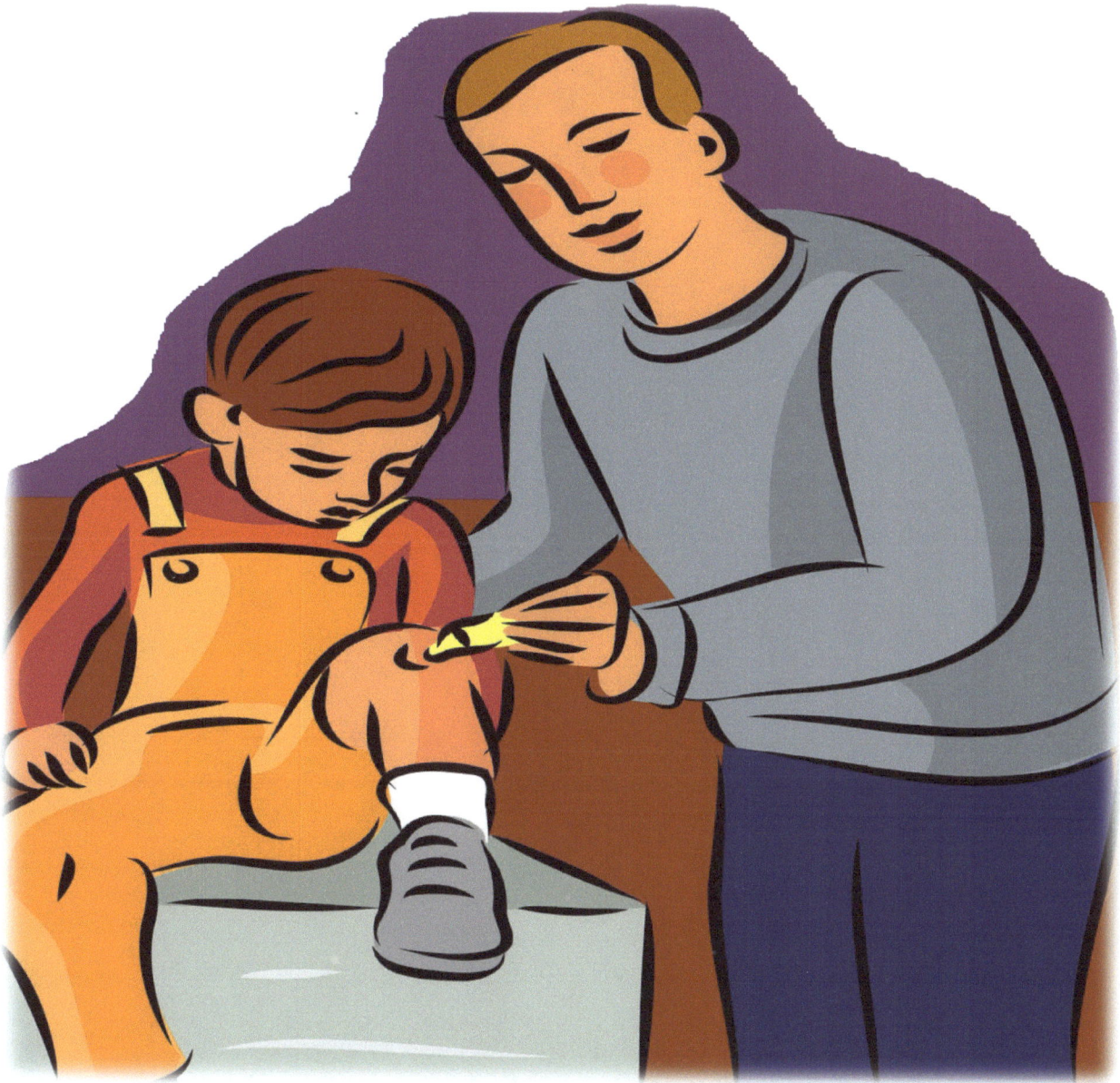

Later that day, my brother came to see me. He looked real sad as he walked in the door. "How are you feeling?" he asked as he sat on the edge of the bed. I gave him a big smile and answered, "I am fine." He rubbed some cream on my wound and said, "Oh yeah, you will get better this time."

That night the nurse woke me up for my medication. She smiled and said, "You're doing well." But I felt really tired and kind of depressed, and I wondered if I should tell her. I asked if my parents were still here and she sadly said, "No." Then she continued, "But you are getting better and this is something they do know."

The very next morning I felt so good. I wanted to jump around and yell with glee. The doctor said, "You need your final shot. Don't worry it will help you a lot." My mother, father, and brother were there, giving me lots of love. I said, "I will get better" and thanked God up above. A smile came over our faces as we headed for the door. I kindly said, "Doctor, I hope I don't see you anymore."

Story 2

I DON'T NEED HELP

I don't need help anymore like I did once before, to open a can or even a door.

I have muscles now you see, from drinking milk and eating my veggies.

I used to have someone feed me my meals, now I do it no big deal.

I used to have someone get a toy off
the shelf, but now I do it by myself.

I can do it, yes, I can. I'm my mommy's little man.

I can do it in a whirl,
I'm my daddy's little girl.

I don't need help, that's what I think, even if I should spill my drink.

I can clean my room super fast,
make my bed and get the trash.

That's no problem for me, you see,
because I am big and help my mommy.

I can do it all now and don't
need help no way, no how.